Fireworks

Dragons, Jungles and Dinosaurs

SKILLS BOOK

Gill & Macmillan
Hume Avenue
Park West
Dublin 12
www.gillmacmillan.ie

ISBN: 9780717152995
© Michael O'Reilly, Caroline Quinn 2012

Design: Outburst Design / Aisli Madden
Cover illustration: Aisli Madden
Inside illustrations: Derry Dillon
Printed and bound in Italy by L.E.G.O. SpA

First published June 2012

Acknowledgements
Poem 'Spaghetti' from *Where the Sidewalk Ends* by Shel Silverstein, ©1981 Evil Eye Music, Inc. and 2009 Evil Eye, LLC, reprinted by permission of David Grossman Literary Agency Ltd. Poem 'Seasick' ©Nick Toczek. Poem 'I Have a Lion' from *Moon, Have You Met My Mother?* by Karla Kuskin, © 2003 HarperCollins Publishers Ltd.

Picture Credits
Illustrations from *Horrid Henry* by Francesca Simon © Tony Ross 1994. Illustrations from *Tiger Lily* by Maeve Friel © Joelle Dreidemy. Reprinted by permission of Stripes Publishing Ltd, 1 the Coda Centre, 189 Munster Road, London, SW6 6AW. Illustrations from *The Pain and the Great One* by Judy Blume © Kate Prankhurst. Reprinted by permission of Macmillan Publishers Ltd, Brunel Road, Houndmills, Basingstoke, Hampshire RG21 6XS. Illustrations from *Dino Egg* by Charlie James © Charlie James. Reprinted by permission of Bloomsbury Publishing Plc. Illustrations from *The Legend of the Worst Boy in the World* by Eoin Colfer © Tony Ross 2007. Illustrations from *Judy Moody Saves the World!* by Megan McDonald, illustrated by Peter H. Reynolds © 2001 Peter H. Reynolds. Reprinted by permission of Walker Books Ltd, London SE11 5HJ www.walker.co.uk. Illustrations from *Utterly Me, Clarice Bean* by Lauren Child © Lauren Child. Reprinted by permission of David Higham Associates Ltd. Illustration from *You're a Bad Man Mr Gum!* by Andy Stanton © David Tazzyman. Reprinted by permission of Egmont UK Ltd, 239 Kensington High Street, London W8 6SA, United Kingdom.

The authors and publisher have made every effort to trace all copyright holders, but if any has been inadvertently overlooked we would be pleased to make the necessary arrangement at the first opportunity.

Contents

An Irish giant

Word bank

short cut terrible roared furious bellowed stooping popped ugly fierce wicked chuckled thumped muddy peered dreadful behold sighed sly dashed scowled twitched frowned chattered measles

A. True or false

Some of these sentences are true, some are false.

Tick the boxes and then rewrite the false sentences correctly in your copybook.

		True	False
1.	The giant's name was Michael Cotter O'Brien.	☐	☐
2.	The Irish Giant was nearly three metres tall.	☐	☐
3.	Patrick went to Paris to seek his fortune.	☐	☐
4.	Patrick often lit his pipe from an electric lamp.	☐	☐
5.	The picture of Patrick with his tailor was drawn by John Kay.	☐	☐

B. An Irish giant

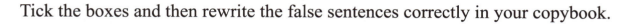

1. Why do you think Patrick Cotter O'Brien would be a good builder?
   _____

2. How did Patrick become rich? _____
   _____

3. How do we know that Patrick was shy? _____
   _____

4. Why did the highwayman get a shock? _____
   _____

5. Why might people have wanted to steal Patrick's body from his grave?_____
   _____

6. What orders did he give to make sure this did not happen?_____
   _____

1

C. Choose a topic
Answer *two* from the list below.

1. The text tells us that Patrick Cotter O'Brien lived about 200 years ago. Do a subtraction sum to find out roughly when he was born.

2. Patrick had two Irish surnames, Cotter and O'Brien. Make a list of other Irish surnames.

3. If your surname is an Irish one, find out what part of Ireland this surname comes from.

4. If your surname is not an Irish one, write a short paragraph explaining where your surname comes from.

- _____
  _____
- _____
  _____

The Little Boy's Secret

A. Discussing and answering questions
Discuss each of these questions with a partner and then choose two of the questions to answer in your copybook.

1. Think of suitable names for the giants in the story.

2. Discuss the words used to describe how the giants moved and spoke. There are lots of these interesting words in the story such as 'twitched' and 'thumped'. Make a list of these words and use them in sentences.

3. What disease did the little boy have? Why were the giants scared?

4. Write about a time when you were sick.

5. Choose one of these paragraph starters to complete.

   - *This story is a bit like...*
   - *My favourite moment in this story is...*
   - *I wonder if...*

6. Make a drawing of the giants' castle. Label the different parts of the castle using these words:

   tower battlements drawbridge moat flags portcullis archway cannon

B. Jumble sale

These sentences are all mixed up. Write them out correctly.

1. The boy mother had a to tell secret his. _____

   _____

2. The hands first hips giant put his on his. _____

   _____

3. The giant pocket the popped shirt boy into his. _____

   _____

4. The ear little boy the whispered in giant's. _____

   _____

5. The knocked giant his over chair. _____

   _____

C. Write a paragraph

1. Choose one of the following topics to write about in your copybook.

   1. Describe a short cut you know.
   2. Find out what 'far-fetched' means. Write three 'far-fetched' sentences.
   3. The giants 'crossed their fingers behind their backs'. What does it mean when a person does that?
   4. Write about another story that has a giant in it.

2. Below is an article taken from *The Fairytale News*, a weekly newspaper in Fairyland. What story is the article about? Write a report on *The Little Boy's Secret* for the newspaper.

NICKED! BIG BAD WOLF ARRESTED IN NIGHTDRESS

IT LOOKS AS THOUGH BB WOLF IS IN BIG TROUBLE AGAIN

Today, shortly after his release from jail on bail, BB Wolf was arrested yet again. BB Wolf had been in jail for blowing down the Little Pigs' houses. This time he is accused of impersonating Granny Hood, locking her in a cupboard, wearing her nightdress and, worst of all, attempting to eat up Little Red Riding Hood.

BB Wolf was found wearing a flowery nightdress, lacy nightcap and spectacles. He claims that it is quite usual for him to wear these things while he is relaxing.

D. Capital work

Definition box

A sentence is a group of words that makes sense. It begins with a capital letter and ends with a full stop.

Example
When we write we should always go back over our work. We can make changes and correct mistakes. This is called editing our work.

1. Add the missing word from the word bank on page 1. Then add capital letters and full stops to the sentences.

1. we took a _____ through the woods to get home quickly

2. the lion _____ loudly

3. i was scared when the bull _____ in the field

4. the popcorn _____ noisily in the microwave

5. my dad _____ when i told him a good joke

6. the monkeys _____ loudly in the treetops

7. i _____ around the corner to see what was there

8. i tried not to scratch when i had the _____

2. Now it's your turn to write sentences leaving out the capital letters and the full stops. Swap copies with a partner and correct each other's sentences.

Definition box

Capital letters are also used for proper nouns – the names of people and places.

3. Circle the words that should start with a capital letter. Write the names of eight places and eight people in the second grid, making sure to give each a capital letter.

dublin	exactly	james	mrs murphy
elephant	london	people	uncle tom
ireland	maybe	margaret	possibly
me	australia	priest	microwave

4. Now use five of these words in sentences of your own.

4

E. Link words

Definition box

Sentences can be joined together using words like and or but. These are link words.

Example
The first giant took the little boy from his pocket. He put him on the kitchen table.
The first giant took the little boy from his pocket and put him on the kitchen table.

1. Join these sentences using and or but and write out the joined sentences.

    1.   Big Bad Wolf leapt straight out of the window. He ran off into the woods.

          _____

    2.   One morning Mrs Hubbard went to the cupboard. The cupboard was bare.

          _____

    3.   Mr Bear put down his morning newspaper. The bears tucked into their porridge.

          _____

    4.   Goldilocks sat in the little chair. She was so heavy that it broke. _____

          _____

    5.   Big Bad Wolf put on Granny Hood's clothes. He hopped into her bed. _____

          _____

    6.   The Queen of Hearts made some tarts. The Knave of Hearts stole them. _____

          _____

2. Draw what happened in one of the sentences above.

F. Speech marks

We're waiting!

1. Read these sentences and fill in the speech
bubbles to show only the words that are spoken.

We can play in
the garden.

Example

'We can play in the garden,' said the little boy.

1. 'I bought the sweets and drinks,'
said Dad.

2. 'It's time to do your homework,'
said Mum.

3. 'Open your books on page seven,'
ordered the teacher.

4. 'Saturday is my favourite day of the
week,' said Ted.

5. 'Christmas Day falls on 25
December,' said Ann.

6. 'Dublin is the capital of Ireland,'
explained the teacher.

2. Illustrate each of these speech bubbles with a character drawing.

What shall we do? We have no food to eat.

You're not really serious.

Not by the hairs on my chinny chin chin, I won't let you in!

Someone has been sleeping in my bed and she's still there!

What big teeth you have!

You must leave the ball before the stroke of midnight.

Magic Bean! I'll give you a magic bean! Throw it away you silly boy.

Take a bite of this lovely, delicious, rosy, red apple my dear!

G. Word treasure hunt

Look at *The Little Boy's Secret* again and find all the words that the author uses instead of said.

1. Write these words on the coins in the pot of gold.

2. Write sentences using each of these words.

_____

_____

_____

_____

_____

My Baby Brother's Secret

Study a poem

Read the poem in your Anthology again and answer the questions.

1. Why are the baby brother's secrets safe? _____

_____

2. Do you have a baby brother or sister? Does he, or she, have any funny little

habits? Write about these._____

_____

3. Why do people think that whispering is sometimes bad manners? _____

_____

4. Have you ever played a game of Chinese Whispers? Write out a set of instructions for this game in your copybook. Ask your teacher if you can play the game in class.

Clever challenges

1. Complete one of these articles for *The Fairytale News*.

   - *The three bears claimed that their porridge was eaten and…*
   - *After searching the length and breadth of Fairyland it has been reported that Prince Charming…*
   - *Young Jack Hubbard has managed to grow…*

2. Write an advertisement for the newspaper.
   Examples

OLD LAMP for sale – *good condition, only one previous owner.* Genuine callers only. Contact Aladdin at 10 Rub A Dub Lane.	**LOST SHEEP** **Reward offered for information that leads to their recovery.** *Contact Bo Peep at bopeep@fairyland.com*	

3. Sometimes authors work with storyboards – which are like cartoon strips. They draw a series of pictures telling the story and write a sentence or two under each picture. They then add more sentences to the story board until the whole story is told. Make a storyboard of your favourite fairytale.

4. Which story character said what? Write out a sentence for three characters using speech marks.

   > **Example**
   > 'I have to get away,' the giant roared.

5. Draw other characters in your copybook and use speech bubbles to show what they are saying (direct speech).

6. For each speech bubble, write a sentence without using speech marks (indirect or reported speech), for example: The giant roared that he had to get away.

7. Use an atlas to find ten interesting place names then write them in your copybook. Add a sentence saying where each place is *or* draw a map of the world to show where they are.

8. Draw a picture of what you imagine one of these places looks like.

The greatest show in the world

A. Circus quiz

Read the circus poster and the ticket in your Anthology again and answer the questions.

1. What is Señor Mendes' act in the circus?_____
   _____

2. Does the ticket allow you into the circus at any time?_____
   _____

3. Write out the meaning of the words 'non-refundable'. _____
   _____

4. Have you ever been to a circus or seen one on TV? Write sentences about three
   characters you have seen, or might see, in a circus._____
   _____
   _____

5. Describe what you think each performer does. _____
   _____

B. Poster design

Design a new poster for the circus in the box below.

Horrid Henry

Word bank

snatched avoided despaired pretended squashed deed hankie radiator overslept whine complain squabble sofa wondered checked comic peel spotless apron laid helpful delicious forehead fudge interrupted aimed spaghetti trickled fuzzy

A. Action words

Definition box

A verb is an action word. Every sentence needs a verb or an action word to make sense.

Example
Then Peter threw the spaghetti.
Mum felt Henry's forehead.

1. Can you remember the verbs that were in these sentences from the story? Use your Anthology to help you. Then fill in the verb lists for Horrid Henry and Perfect Peter.

---

1. When Horrid Henry's parents took Henry to school they _____ behind him.

2. Children pointed at Henry and _____ to their parents.

3. Perfect Peter always _____ 'please' and 'thank you'.

4. Peter never, ever _____ his nose.

5. Henry continued _____ Peter's crayons on the radiator.

6. Henry did not wake Peter by _____ water on Peter's head.

7. Henry did not _____ with Peter over who sat in front.

8. Dad _____ to see if a comic was hidden inside the book.

9. Peter _____ his spotless hands.

10. Peter _____ up his plate and _____ it at Henry.

Make a 'Horrid Henry' verb list		Make a 'Perfect Peter' verb list	
snatched		loved	

2. Make up sentences using three of your 'Horrid Henry' verbs and three of your 'Perfect Peter' verbs.

> **Example**
> Henry always snatched toys from the other children.
> Peter loved to help his parents at home.

1. _____

2. _____

3. _____

1. _____

2. _____

3. _____

B. Opposites

Here are some word opposites. These types of words are called antonyms. Find the opposite of each word in the first box by rearranging the letters of the words in the second box.

tall	ounyg
wide	dne
light	rdah
begin	radk
old	rrnawo
night	sorht short
happy	mean
generous	das
soft	yda

Now write sentences in your copybook using your word pairs.

> **Example**
> The motorway is wide but the lane is narrow.

12

C. Asking questions

Definition box

When we write a question, we use a special sign called a
question mark at the end of the sentence. It looks like this: ?

Example
'What are we going to do about
that horrible boy?' sighed Mum.

1. Find eight questions in the story. Write them here. (Don't forget the
   question marks.)

   1. _____
   2. _____
   3. _____
   4. _____
   5. _____
   6. _____
   7. _____
   8. _____

2. In the bubbles below and overleaf write one question you would like to ask
   each of these people.

favourite author

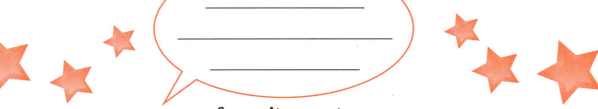

favourite pop star

favourite TV star

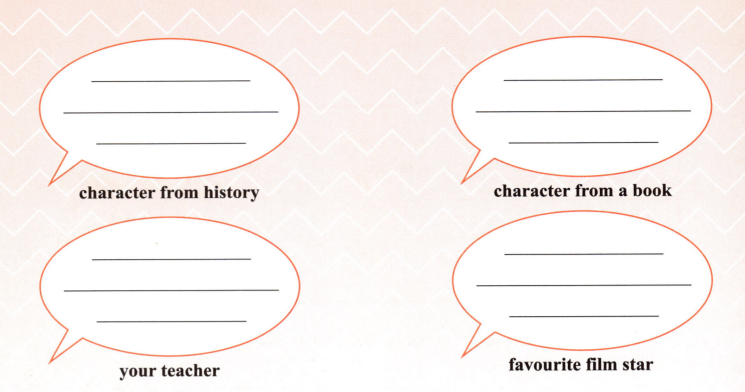

character from history

character from a book

your teacher

favourite film star

D. Lists

1. Peter had good manners. Henry had bad manners. What do you think are good manners? What do you think are bad manners? Make two lists.

Good manners	Bad manners

2. Draw up two lists in your copybook of:
    (a) food which is good for you
    (b) food which is not good for you.

E. A horrid quiz

1.   Someone has mixed up the questions and the answers. Sort them out and write the questions and the correct answers into your copybook.

■ Who was the horrid person in the family?
He was called Peter.
■ What was Horrid Henry's brother's name?
Peter did.
■ Who threw the spaghetti at mum?
Henry was.

2.   Answer the following questions about *Horrid Henry*.

1. How did Henry usually wake Peter up?

      _____

      _____

2. Add to the list of horrid things that Henry might do.
Henry threw food. Henry snatched. Henry pushed and shoved and pinched. Henry... _____

      _____

      _____

3. Do the same for Peter starting with,
Peter always said please and thank you. Peter loved vegetables. Peter always used a hanky and never picked his nose. Peter... _____

      _____

      _____

      _____

4. Do you like 'naughty' or 'horrid' characters in stories? Write a few sentences about one that you know, for example, Dennis the Menace.

      _____

      _____

      _____

5. Write about a time when you could 'stand it no longer'.

      _____

      _____

      _____

6. List five ways of being polite.

      _____

      _____

      _____

      _____

      _____

F. Word trap – are/our

Sometimes we fall into word traps when we are not sure what word to use.

are   our

1. Complete these sentences by adding are or our.

1. The three witches _____ living in that old castle.
2. Our neighbour does not like it when we climb over _____ fence into his garden.
3. 'We _____ going to practise writing letters today,' _____ teacher said.
4. _____ class went on a school trip to Dublin Zoo.
5. _____ favourite games are football and hurling.
6. When _____ you coming to visit _____ school?
7. We _____ back at school and _____ holidays _____ over.
8. Henry and Peter _____ brothers.
9. The teacher puts _____ paintings up on the noticeboard.
10. The school inspector is visiting _____ school to see _____ work.

2. Write three sentences that contain the word 'are' and three sentences that contain the word 'our'.

_____

_____

_____

_____

_____

_____

3. Make a list of other words that can be confusing, for example, of/off , there/their. Write these pairs.

_____   _____

_____   _____

_____   _____

Spaghetti

Shel Silverstein

Spaghetti, Spaghetti, all over the place,
Up to my elbows – up to my face,
Over the carpet and under the chairs,
Into the hammock and wound round the stairs,
Filling the bathtub and covering the desk,
Making the sofa a mad mushy mess.

The party is ruined, I'm terribly worried,
The guests have all left (unless they're all buried).
I told them, 'Bring presents.' I said, 'Throw confetti...'
I guess they heard wrong
'Cause they all threw SPAGHETTI!

1. Read the poem above and then choose two of the following activities to do.

   1. Write an acrostic poem with the title SPAGHETTI.
   2. Draw a picture of the scene at the end of the party.
   3. Make a list of the most horrible things you could throw at a party.
   4. Find and write out a recipe that has spaghetti as an ingredient.
   5. Find the names of different kinds of pasta and list them.

2. Write two short pieces describing how Henry and Peter were opposites.

3. In your copybook draw a portrait of each character. Use any art materials you like.

4. Henry was reading a story about super mice. What do you think this story was about? Work on your own or with a partner to write the story. Start with a plan: Draw the grid below into your copybook and answer all the questions. Then write up your story.

Who is in the story?	What happens in the story?	Why?	Where does it take place?	When does it take place?

5. As a reporter, who would you like to interview in this story? Write out the questions you would like to ask. Ask a partner to pretend to be that person and answer the questions.

6. Choose one scene from the story *Horrid Henry*, draw this scene and add speech bubbles to show what the characters are saying.

Birthdays around the world

Birthday bash quiz

1. Make a list of the sweets you would like to see in a piñata for your birthday.

   _____

   _____

2. Name the birthdays that are important in Nigeria. Which birthdays do we consider more important than others? _____

   _____

   _____

3. What would you eat for lunch on your birthday in China?

   _____

   _____

4. Make up a nice birthday greeting to write inside a birthday card.

   _____

   _____

5. Are you named after a saint? Find out your name-day! _____

   _____

6. In Denmark, birthday children have flags outside their houses to celebrate their birthdays. Design a special birthday flag for yourself.

7. Find out, and write down, how to say 'Happy Birthday' in other languages and compare what you have learned with a partner. _____

   _____

   _____

At My Birthday Party

A. Write a recipe

There are lots of different kinds of cakes in the poem 'At My Birthday Party'. Name other kinds of cakes you know here. Find a recipe for your favourite cake and write it down in your copybook.

B. Stummer cake

In the poem the poet gets 'stummer cake' from eating too much. What other kinds of 'cake' might you have, for example, 'toot cake'? Make a funny list of these.

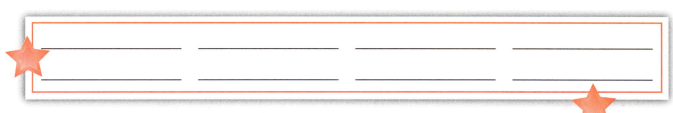

Happy Dogday

A. Feel like a dog

Read the poem 'Happy Dogday'. Now write a paragraph that begins like this:

As I read the poem I felt...

_____

_____

_____

_____

_____

B. Dog diary

From reading the poem you can you see all the different things that Fred loves to do. In your copybook write a diary entry for Fred that begins as follows:

My name is Fred. I am a dog. Today I scratched and played...

Sunkaissa the Golden-haired Princess

 Word bank

traditional seized overcome despair daughter clutches valley stream glanced recognise tune cowshed enormous gigantic dashed mooed million shivered shaky drooped mutter flopped overjoyed imagine

A. The printer's mistake

OOPS! The printer has made a mistake and given you the answers instead of the questions! Write out the questions. Don't forget the question marks.

1. She was golden-haired. _____

2. This story comes from Nepal. _____

3. He sang her a song that they had learned when they were younger. _____
   _____

4. He lost count because the cow gave a great shaky shiver._____
   _____

5. He hid in the cowshed._____

B. Alphabetics

1. Discuss where you find alphabetical lists. Write some places where they are found in this grid.

Dictionary			

2. Put this list of comic book characters into alphabetical order.

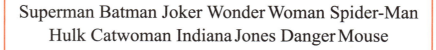

> Superman Batman Joker Wonder Woman Spider-Man
> Hulk Catwoman Indiana Jones Danger Mouse

_____ _____ _____ _____ _____

_____ _____ _____ _____ _____

3. Put the words in each line into alphabetical order.

1. lion	lemon	last
_____	_____	_____
2. flowers	frost	family
_____	_____	_____
3. rain	run	rice
_____	_____	_____
4. monkey	man	mice
_____	_____	_____
5. snake	sand	sit
_____	_____	_____
6. turtle	top	tank
_____	_____	_____
7. animal	acrobat	ask
_____	_____	_____
8. picnic	parcel	post
_____	_____	_____

C. Dictionary

1. Choose ten words from the word bank on page 20. Look them up in the dictionary and write their meanings here.

daughter	A female child

2. Now choose words from the word bank to complete these sentences.

1. The musician played a _____ on his fiddle.

2. You will often find a _____ between two mountains.

3. The cow _____ in the _____.

4. I was so tired that I _____ on my bed and fell asleep.

5. I did not _____ you with your new hairstyle!

6. I was _____ to see all my cousins at the party.

7. I _____ with fright on the ghost train.

3. Rewrite the sentences in your copybook and put a different word in each blank space.

D. Character web

 Definition box

People in a story are called the characters. A character web is a list of all the things we know about a character.

1. Here is a character web for Sunkaissa. Some of it has been done but you have to finish it.

Home
_____
_____

Name
_____
_____

Family
brother
_____

Appearance
beautiful
_____

2. Describe Sunkaissa in your own words.

_____

_____

_____

_____

E. Word trap – of/off

Here are two other words that we sometimes mix up.

| of | off |

> **Example**
> There was no sign of his sister.
> The brother dashed off to the cowshed.

1. See if you can use them correctly.

1. The monster took Sunkaissa _____ to his cave.

2. The people loved hearing the story _____ the cow.

3. The people _____ the village welcomed Sunkaissa home.

4. _____ he went, following the stream.

5. The door _____ the cowshed crashed open.

6. The monster dozed _____ while counting the cow's hairs.

2. Correct the mistakes in these sentences and rewrite them.

1. We are going of to visit our cousins tomorrow. _____

_____

2. People love to listen to stories off monsters. _____

_____

3. The people off a country are its citizens. _____

_____

4. 'Of we go on our holidays,' said Dad. _____

_____

5. The bottom rung off the ladder was broken. _____

_____

6. I dozed of while I was watching TV. _____

_____

Clever challenges

1. You have already created a character web for Sunkaissa. Now create a character web in your copybook for a different character you have come across in this book, or a character from another book you have read.

2. This is a folktale from *Nepal*. What do you know about Nepal?
   Fill in a KWL chart in your copybook to begin with and then use your library and the Internet to help with your research.

K What I know	W What I want to know	L What I have learned

3. What other stories include monsters? Make a list of these monsters and the books they feature in.

4. Write out the words of a song or a poem that you learned when you were very young and draw a picture to go with it.

5. Sunkaissa is described as *golden-haired*. If her hair were a different colour how might she have been described? Write five other descriptions beginning like this:
   Sunkaissa was dark-haired...

6. Find and read a traditional story from another country. Write the story in a few sentences and draw pictures to illustrate it.

7. Find information about cows and write out ten facts you have learned about them.

8. Try putting this list of characters from storybooks into alphabetical order.

> Rumpelstiltskin Red Riding Hood Cinderella Jack
> Beauty Snow White Dorothy Aladdin Thumbelina

9. Make up a list of your own and ask a partner to put it into alphabetical order.

10. Put the words in the word bank at the beginning of this chapter into alphabetical order.

The Whales' Song

Word bank

jetty perfect stomped daft snapped blubber nonsense cavemen magical grumbled ocean dusk foolishness awoke distance shore enormous spun extinct baleen sperm beluga humpback mammal

A. More errors

This time the silly author forgot to finish the questions! Put in the missing words and then give the questions to a friend to write the answers.

1. How did Uncle Frederick _____?

_____

2. Where did Lilly _____?

_____

3. Can you describe _____?

_____

4. What were the whales _____?

_____

B. A whale of a time

Have you read books, seen TV programmes or watched films about whales? Write five things you already know about whales, five things you would like to know and then five things you have learned after reading the story in your Anthology.

K What I know	W What I want to know	L What I have learned

C. Missing words

1.   Complete the following paragraph using the most suitable words. When you have finished compare with the same paragraph in your Anthology to see how well you did.

> Next morning Lilly _____ down to the ocean. _____ went where no one fished _____ swam or sailed _____ boats. She _____ to the end of the old jetty, the _____ was empty and _____. Out of her pocket she took _____ yellow _____ and dropped it _____ the water.

2.   Now choose a paragraph from a story you have already read in your Anthology. Write it out in your copybook leaving out some words. Ask your partner to complete it.

D. More missing words

1.   Fill in the blank spaces in these sentences using words from the word bank on page 25.

- Lilly's Uncle Frederick _____ into the room.
- She could hear something in the _____, on the far side of the hill.
- They were the most _____ creatures you could ever imagine.
- Next morning Lilly went down to the _____.
- That night, Lilly _____ suddenly.

2.   In your copybook, rewrite these sentences putting words of your own into the blank spaces.

E. Comparisons

1.   When we compare things we often use the words like or as. Find two examples from *The Whales' Song* and write them here.

> _____
>
> _____
>
> _____

2.   Now fill in the missing words in these sentences.
Mum was as busy as a _____ preparing food for my party. The kitten, bold as _____, sneaked in and ate the cocktail sausages. She left muddy footprints all over the tablecloth which had been as white as _____. The dog who was always as good as _____ crept up behind her, as quiet as a _____ and chased her away.

3.   Make up your own comparisons and use six of them in sentences.

eat like	swim like
as cold as	as big as
shine like	jump like
as pretty as	as tiny as
walk like	drive like
as clever as	as warm as

_____

_____

_____

_____

_____

_____

F.   Be a poet

Write a short poem using as many comparisons as you can just like the example below.
Illustrate your poem. Collect all your poems together and make a class book of poetry.

ELEPHANT

As big as a whale
As tall as a house
Legs like tree stumps
Walks like a bulldozer
Trunk like a vacuum cleaner
Loud as a foghorn
In the forest

G. Singular and plural

Definition box

Nouns can be singular or plural. Singular means one and plural means more than one.
Sometimes we add s to mean more than one.

| **Example** one dog – two dogs. |

Sometimes we have to add es.

| **Example** one box – two boxes. |

1. Fill in the plurals in these sentences.
   - ■ I have one book on my desk, but you have two _____ on your desk.
   - ■ Put the sick animal in the shed and drive all the other _____ out into the field.
   - ■ I would not mind meeting one giant, but meeting lots of _____ might be scary.
   - ■ Casper is a friendly ghost but other_____ are not so friendly.
   - ■ Most _____ are big but the blue whale is enormous.
   - ■ Very small schools sometimes have only one class. Most schools have two or more _____.
   - ■ Put the big dish in the sink and the smaller _____ in the dishwasher.
   - ■ We go to the beach sometimes but in warm countries _____ are usually crowded.

2. Put these sentences into the plural and write them in your copybook. Watch out! You may have to change other words in the sentences as well as adding s or es.

   > **Example**
   > The fox was asleep in his den. The foxes *were* asleep in *their* dens.

   - ■ The teacher told me to put my book away in my bag.
   - ■ My favourite animal in the zoo is the elephant.
   - ■ I dressed up as a ghost on Halloween.
   - ■ The last coach leaves the station at twelve o'clock.
   - ■ Put a knife and fork beside each dish.
   - ■ A ghost lives in that old house.
   - ■ I bought a brand new axe.

3. Work out a rule that will help you to remember when to add es to change from singular to plural.

_____

_____

Whales

A. Whale search

1. Fill in the missing words in the sentences below, then circle or colour in the answers in the word maze. After you have finished, check in the *Whales* piece in your Anthology to see how well you have done.

A whale is not a fish, it is a _____.

The thick layer of fat under a whale's skin is called _____.

A whale breathes air in through a _____ on top of its head.

Whales with no teeth are called _____.

The _____ whale is the largest creature on earth.

_____ is an organisation that tries to protect whales.

The _____ whale is a speedy swimmer and a fierce hunter.

The _____ whale is sometimes called the 'sea canary'.

The whale that dives to the ocean floor to feed is the _____ whale.

The _____ whale is very curious and playful.

Whales often live in groups called _____.

Whales can _____ to each other under the water.

M	B	L	U	B	B	E	R	K	S
A	L	W	P	A	L	A	W	I	P
M	O	O	O	L	U	T	H	L	E
M	W	U	D	E	E	A	A	L	R
A	H	L	S	E	T	M	L	E	M
L	O	D	O	N	O	E	E	R	I
T	L	H	U	M	P	B	A	C	K
O	E	L	O	V	E	H	A	V	E
G	R	E	E	N	P	E	A	C	E
B	E	L	U	G	A	T	A	L	K

2. The letters in the word maze that you have not used make up another set of words.
Use these to make a sentence and write it below.

_____

_____

29

B. Whale fact file

From what you have read about whales in your Anthology complete the next two exercises.

1. Answer the following questions using full sentences.

1. What are whales? _____
    _____

2. What is the fat on a whale's body called? _____
    _____

3. How do whales breathe?_____
    _____

4. What are whales with no teeth called? _____
    _____

5. How do whales communicate?_____
    _____

6. Why did humans hunt whales in the past? _____
    _____

7. Are whales safe from hunting now?_____
    _____

2. Write two facts about each type of whale in the table below. Research a whale not mentioned in the Anthology and write two facts about it in the last box.

Blue whale	Sperm whale	Killer whale
Beluga	Humpback	

C. Playing with words

Writers love to play with words. In this poem the poet plays with the names of creatures that live in the ocean to tell us a funny story about a sick squid.

Seasick

Nick Toczek

'I don't feel whelk,' whaled the squid, sole-fully.
'What's up?' asked the doctorpus.
'I've got sore mussels and a tummy hake,' she told him.

'Lie down and I'll egg salmon you,' mermaid the doctorpus.
'Rays your voice,' said the squid. 'I'm a bit hard of herring.'
'Sorry I didn't do it on porpoise,' replied the doctorpus orc-wardly.

He helped her to oyster self onto his couch
And asked her to look up so he could sea urchin.
He soon flounder plaice that hurt.

'This'll make it eel,' he said whiting a prescription.
'So I won't need to see the sturgeon?' she asked.
'Oh, no,' he told her. 'In a couple of dace you'll feel brill.'

'Cod bless you,' she said.
'That'll be sick squid,' replied the doctorpus.

Make a list of the ocean creatures that feature in the poem.

_____
_____
_____
_____
_____
_____
_____
_____
_____
_____
_____
_____
_____
_____
_____

1. Answer these questions (in the style of the poet).

   1. How did the squid say she felt? _____
   2. Has the squid got good hearing? _____
   3. What did the doctorpus help the squid to do? _____
   4. What did he find? _____
   5. What did the doctorpus 'white'? _____
   6. How much was the bill? _____

2. In your copybook, rewrite the poem using ordinary language.

D. The blue whale

For every blue whale alive today there were once 20. People hunted and killed so many of them that fewer than 10,000 remain. Blue whales are now protected and hunting them is banned, so in some places their numbers are growing – but very, very slowly. You could still sail the oceans for a year and never see a single one.

Read the two descriptions below.

The blue whale is big.

Bigger than a giraffe.

Bigger than an elephant.

Bigger than a dinosaur.

The blue whale is the biggest creature that has ever lived on earth!

Blue whales can grow to over 30 metres long and weigh 140 tonnes – that's heavier than 25 elephants or 115 giraffes. Female blue whales are usually a little bigger than the males.

1. Compare the two descriptions. Which do you prefer? Write down the reasons for your choice.

_____

_____

_____

2. Answer the following questions using the information in your Anthology and in the boxes above.

1. How many elephants would weigh the same as a blue whale? _____

   _____

2. How do blue whales find their way around in the deep? _____

   _____

3. How is the blue whale similar to humans? _____

   _____

4. For how long can a blue whale stay under water? _____

   _____

5. How many krill can a blue whale eat in one day? _____

   _____

Clever challenges

1. Make a list of all the creatures you know that live in the ocean.

2. Choose three of these creatures and do some research on them. Then write a paragraph about each one and add a picture.

3. Imagine that you have been asked to write the information piece about whales in a different way. You can present it as a fact map, an illustrated diagram or in any other way you like. Use the information you already have or do more research to produce a new piece for your Anthology.

4. Some girls, like Lilly, are named after flowers. Write a list of other girls' names that are also flowers.

5. Lilly's grandmother loved the whales, they were special to her. But what did they do all day?
   Imagine you are a baby whale and write about a day in your life in your diary – write about what you did, what you saw, what you ate, an exciting event that happened to you, etc. You could plan this on a mind map. Write a rough draft in your copybook to start with, edit this by making any changes and then write your final draft.

6. Write a play based on the poem 'Seasick' in your copybook.
   Start like this:
   Squid: I don't feel whelk!
   Doctorpus: What's up?
   Squid: I've got...

7. Read the poem 'The Song of the Whale'. How did this poem make you feel? Now write a paragraph to complete one of these starters.

   ■ *I was shocked by...*

   ■ *As I read the poem I felt...*

   ■ *I was sorry that...*

Tiger Lily: A Heroine in the Making

Word bank

roared inflatable suffering magnets mobile regulars rucksacks volumes paperbacks obsessed mysterious ingenious countless companion devoted appearance nervous mused clamped yowling governess steering canoe choked rainforest slaloming

A. True or false

		True	False
1.	Lily's dog is called Lassie.	☐	☐
2.	She lives with her mum Vicky.	☐	☐
3.	Lily decided to become a night errant.	☐	☐
4.	Mum roared at Lily from the bottom of the stairs.	☐	☐
5.	Lily sellotaped poems to doors and walls.	☐	☐
6.	Lily's mother drove the mobile library.	☐	☐
7.	Lily dug up the garden looking for jewels after reading *Treasure Island*.	☐	☐
8.	Auntie Pamela's hair salon is called 'Curl Up & Dye'.	☐	☐

B. Book types

1. Lily is mad about books. Her house is full of them. There are lots of different types. Examine the different types of books in your class or school library.
Complete the table.

Type of book	Meaning
Fairytale	
Detective	
Adventure	
Science Fiction	
Mystery	
Picture	

2.　What is your favourite type of book? List the best books you have read so far.

_____　_____

_____　_____

_____　_____

3.　Write a review of a book you are reading at the moment.

My book review

_____

_____

_____

_____

_____

_____

_____

_____

_____

C.　Help!

The author has lost the Anthology and cannot remember
the details of the story. Help the author by crossing out the
wrong words.

1.　Lily had a *dog/cat* named *Bosie/Rosie*.
2.　Lots of people in Lily's village are *stupid/weird*.
3.　Lily plans to become a *King/Queen/Knight* Errant.
4.　Everyone called Lily *Lion/Tiger/Cheetah*.
5.　Lily had always been mad about *comics/books/magazines*.
6.　There was an inflatable *elephant/giraffe/octopus* under the stairs.
7.　Lily loved to sellotape *photos/letters/poems* to the doors and walls.
8.　Lily's mum drove a mobile *shop/library/ice-cream van*.
9.　Fern rescued a little *rabbit/pig/monkey* in *Charlotte's Web*.
10.　Lily's favourite book was *Alice in Wonderland/Charlotte's Web/Little Women*.

D. My favourite poem

Information about my favourite poem.

Type: _____

Title: _____

Author: _____

Reason: _____

_____

_____

E. Characters from famous books

1. Lily's favourite books all have interesting characters. Complete this list.

Title of Book	Character	Action
Charlotte's Web	Fern	Rescues Wilbur
Alice in Wonderland		
Pippi Longstocking		
The Secret Garden		
Little Women		

2. Choose one of the following to complete.

- ■ *I really liked the character of Tiger Lily because…*

- ■ *I did not like the character of Tiger Lily because…*

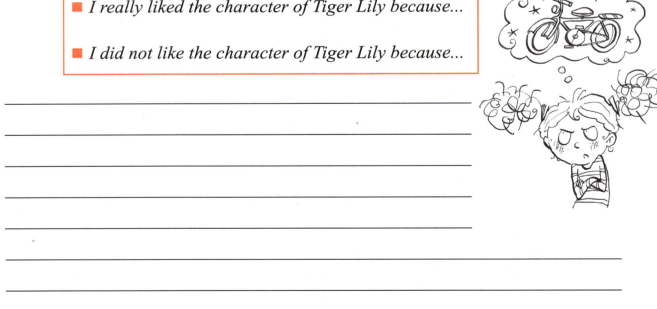

_____

_____

_____

_____

_____

_____

_____

F. Make a map

Do you think it is a good idea for an author to have a map in a story? Why do you think so? Draw a map of where you live here.

 Clever challenges

1. Make a small book with paper and card (for the cover). Use cartoons, speech bubbles and your own writing to tell the story!
   Finish your book with the line 'Isn't it great when a plan comes together!'

   > I'm going to become a **Superhero**, and this is how I am going to do it!

2. Use the map in the story to help you write out the directions from Lily's house to Cow Lane. Be as clear as you can.

3. Choose a story or a nursery rhyme. Draw a map of the area where the action/story takes place.

4. You have a new job as an auctioneer. Someone wants to buy a site for a new house. Write a description of a place called 'The Middle of Nowhere'.
   Persuade your client that this is THE place to build a house.

5. Tiger Lily said she needed a 'trusty companion'. Do you have a good friend like that? Who is it? What kind of things do you share with them? Write a paragraph about this companion.

Irish musical instruments

A. Music quiz

Answer these questions as full sentences.

1. How old is the oldest harp in Ireland? _____
   _____

2. Who was the most famous Irish harpist? _____
   _____

3. What does the Irish word *uilleann* mean? _____
   _____

4. What is a lament? _____
   _____

5. What animal's skin is used to make a *bodhrán*? _____
   _____

B. Music around the world

How well do you know your musical instruments? Use the following list of words to fill in the gaps in these sentences. You may have to use a dictionary or a book about music to help you!

> piano xylophone didgeridoo ukulele cymbals trumpet violin

1. A _____ is a small guitar often played in Hawaii.

2. Another name for the fiddle is the _____.

3. In Australia the Aborigine people play the _____.

4. The _____ are part of a drum kit.

5. You play the _____ by hitting the keys with sticks.

6. The keys of a _____ were made from ivory in the past.

7. You blow into wind instruments such as the _____.

C. Listen and respond

Listen to any piece of music and make a list of all the instruments that you can hear.

D. Favourite music

Choose your favourite singer, band or group and write a short paragraph about them here.

_____

_____

_____

_____

_____

_____

_____

_____

_____

_____

_____

_____

_____

_____

_____

_____

_____

_____

_____

_____

E. Word trap – do/does

Here are two words that we sometimes mix up.

| do | does |

> **Example**
> Mary and John do their homework together.
> Mary does not like brushing her teeth.

1. Now see if you can use them correctly.

1. The giants _____ not like the little boy.
2. Peter _____ a lot of work in the house.
3. Jim and Joe are brothers but they still _____ not like each other.
4. We _____ not like homework but our teacher _____.

Here are two other words that we sometimes mix up.

| did | done |

> **Example**
> 'Where did you get that super dress?' asked Mary.
> 'Have you done all your homework?' asked the teacher.

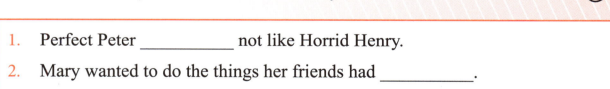

2. Now see if you can use them correctly.

1. Perfect Peter _____ not like Horrid Henry.
2. Mary wanted to do the things her friends had _____.
3. I _____ my homework at the kitchen table.
4. The youngest prince _____ not want to do what his brothers had _____.

3. Now write sentences of your own using *do, does, did* and *done*.

_____

_____

_____

_____

The Giggler Treatment

Word bank

boring perfectly measuring tonsils ninja surrounded adults forward mumbling stripes vulture swooped shock flask yapping interesting favourite nodded

A. Cracker facts

The cream crackers were always yapping. They had the most *boring* things to say.

Babies are smaller than adults...

A car has four wheels but a bike has only two...

Toilet paper is usually white but not always...

Write ten of your own facts but make them *interesting* – not like the cream crackers!

1. _____
2. _____
3. _____
4. _____
5. _____
6. _____
7. _____
8. _____
9. _____
10. _____

B. Tasty!

Mister Mack had the boring job of tasting cream crackers.
Would you like to be a taster? Finish these sentences.

1. If I were a biscuit taster I would like to taste_____.
2. If I were a sweet taster I would like_____.
3. If I were a fruit taster _____.
4. If I were a cereal taster _____.
5. If I were a drinks taster _____.
6. If I were a_____.
7. If I were a_____.

C. What a boring job

What do you think are boring jobs? What are exciting ones? Add to the lists below.

Boring jobs	Exciting jobs
cream cracker taster	Superhero

Greedy Dog

Making lists

Read the poem 'Greedy Dog' in your Anthology and complete the following exercises.

1. Why do you think the dog will not eat mushrooms and cucumber?

_____

_____

2. Add to the lists of things that you think the dog will and will not eat.

Things the dog will eat	Things the dog will not eat
apple cores	mushrooms
bacon fat	cucumber
the cat's milk	
hot buttered toast	

Clever challenges

1. The fig rolls never talked when Mr Mack was asleep. That was why he liked them. If they had talked, what would they have said? Write a few of their comments in your copybook.

2. How do they get the figs into the fig rolls? Write your explanation.

3. Some parts of this story are very far-fetched. Choose five of them and finish these paragraph starters.

   1. *I don't believe that... because...*
   2. *It is very far-fetched that... because...*
   3. *It is not likely that... because...*
   4. *You would be mad to think that... because...*
   5. *There is no way that... because...*

4. The Mack brothers, Jimmy and Robbie, were playing football when they broke the window. Imagine you were the reporter at the scene. Write a report of the match. Read your report to the class.

5. The second poem in this unit is 'Roger the Dog' by Ted Hughes. Have you heard of this famous poet before? Look through poetry books or anthologies to find more of his poems. Copy one out, make an illustration for it and read it aloud to your class. Use the Internet and a search engine to help you do this.

A. Road signs

What do each of these road signs mean?

This road sign means

_____

This road sign means

_____

This road sign means

_____

This road sign means

_____

This road sign means

_____

This road sign means

_____

This road sign means

_____

This road sign means

_____

B. Label the diagram

Here is a picture of a motorbike. Label the different parts in the same way the bicycle in your Anthology is labelled.

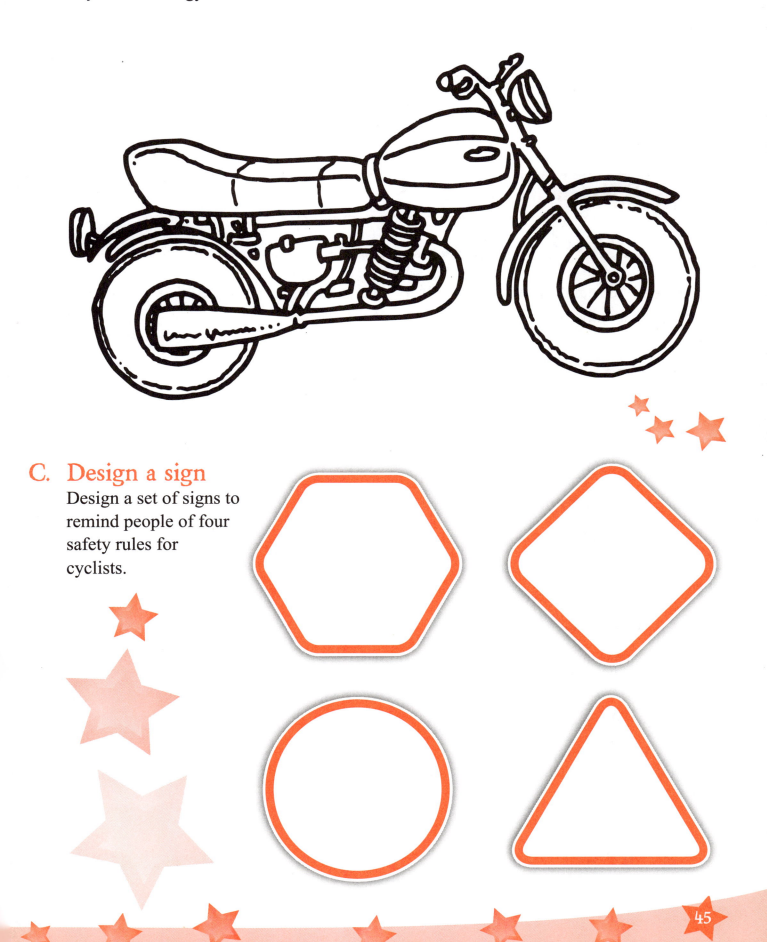

C. Design a sign

Design a set of signs to remind people of four safety rules for cyclists.

Oh, Woe Ith Me!

Report

Write the poem in everyday language.

As I was biking down the street _____

I crashed _____

My bike is _____

The Pain and the Great One: Soupy Saturdays

Word bank

pretended repeated cartwheel positively padded wrist guards waddled glimpse
reminded steady pumping wobbly balance ordinary

A. Missing words

Complete these sentences without looking in your Anthology. When you have finished check back to see how close your endings were to the author's.

1. Mom called, 'Who wants _____ '

2. 'Actually', Aunt Diana said, 'the baby is _____ '

3. 'What does maths have to _____ ' I asked.

4. I can jump rope, turn an almost-perfect cartwheel and make _____

5. This will positively, absolutely be _____

6. I was so padded I _____

7. Close your eyes and *feel* _____

8. Mitchell ran, holding _____

9. Pedal, brake, _____

10. You could have a boring, ordinary sister. Instead, _____

B. Adverbs

Definition box

An adverb tells us more about a verb. The author of this story uses adverbs to tell us more about the verbs.

Example
He talks gently.
I pedalled quickly.

1. Use your Anthology to complete the following sentences.

   1. Mitchell hardly ever says anything. When he does, he talks very

      _____.

   2. You have to listen _____ or you'll miss what he is saying.

   3. So I started to pedal, I pedalled very, very _____.

   4. This will _____, _____, be my final try.

2. Look through your book and find six other adverbs. Make an adverb list.

3. Put each adverb into a sentence to show you know the meaning of the word.

_____

_____

_____

_____

_____

_____

C. That was hard!

Write a short paragraph about something that you found difficult to learn. Describe how you eventually learned to do this and who helped you.

_____

_____

_____

_____

_____

D. Dictionary work

Use the dictionary to check the meaning of these words. Then complete the table.

Words	Meaning
padding	
glimpse	
pretended	
scooped	
ordinary	
cartwheel	
whizzed	
positively	
brake	

E. Speech marks

Put the missing speech marks into the following sentences. Then look back to *The Pain and the Great One* to check your work.

1. I do Dad answered.
2. Abigail he said louder.
3. What does maths have to do with riding a bike? I asked.
4. I'm good at maths I told him.
5. Yes you can Mitchell said.
6. I always fall when I stop I told him.
7. Who says I'm glad he asked.

 Clever challenges

1. In this story we read that some people find maths hard to do. Make up a problem-solving plan in four easy steps. Ask your friends to try it out and see if it helps to solve a problem.

2. Draw a pictogram showing how all the pupils in your class travel to school.

3. Write a set of instructions with pictures for one of the following:
   - Making a sandwich
   - Playing a game of your choice
   - Staying safe on your bike
   - Setting the table.

4. Mitchell is not very happy with the Pain. He wants to tell him just what he thinks of him. You are his speech writer. Write the speech he will give to the Pain start with 'Now listen here you…'

5. Find a partner to act as the Pain. Ask her/him to reply to your speech.

TV guide

A. TV quiz

Answer the following questions using full sentences.

1. Which animal has its own documentary? _____
   _____

2. Who are the hosts of *Game Show*? _____
   _____

3. What Irish band will play during *The Saturday Show*? _____
   _____

4. What is the topic on *Question Time*? _____
   _____

5. On which programme do you think you will see pyramids? _____
   _____

6. On what show will you see acrobats? _____
   _____

7. What type of film is *Galaxy Battle*? _____
   _____

8. Who will be interviewed on *Space Documentary*? _____
   _____

B. TV schedule

Pretend that you are the programme manager at a TV station. Make out a most exciting TV schedule for an evening's viewing with all your favourite programmes on it.

4p.m.	
5p.m.	
6p.m.	
7p.m.	
8p.m.	
9p.m.	
10p.m.	

C. Catchy titles

Some of the names of the TV programmes listed in your Anthology are boring. People often watch a programme because it has a 'catchy' title. Imagine that you are the presenter of some of these programmes, make up really interesting titles for them.

Original title	New title
Nature Trail	'Adventures in the Wild' with (your name)
News	'The World in Action' with...

D. Word trap

1. Choose **is** or **are** to complete these sentences.

> 1. Mum's anti-wrinkle cream _____ on her <u>dressing table</u>.
>
> 2. The can of de-icer spray _____ in the <u>boot</u> of the car.
>
> 3. It is very bright! Where _____ my <u>sunglasses</u>?
>
> 4. There _____ lots of dead <u>daddy-long-legs</u> in the spider's web.
>
> 5. My slinky toy _____ broken, it will not go down the <u>stairs</u>.
>
> 6. There _____ lots of seeds in this <u>packet</u>.
>
> 7. The teacher's <u>whistle</u> _____ broken.
>
> 8. I need to open this tin of <u>beans</u>. _____ the tin opener in that drawer?

2. Rewrite the sentences in your copybook, replacing the underlined word with a new one.

3. Write five sentence pairs like these in your copybook:
   Here **is** one loaf of brown bread. Here **are** two loaves of white bread.
   There **is** one time capsule buried here. There **are** five capsules buried over there.

The Winter Hedgehog

Word bank

misty undergrowth overheard determined swiftly swooped countryside emerged slugs insects roosts burrows warrens straggling sparkled prickles scurried sped slinking riverbank rumble belly pounced sly reeled blizzard moaned shelter enchanted pebbles admired nibbled munched blinked tumbled cloak larders sleighs stoat crocuses snowdrops yawn sigh snore

A. Be a reporter

1.   Today you are a reporter for the school newspaper. Your job is to interview the winter hedgehog. Read the story again and write down the questions you want to ask. Find a partner to be the hedgehog and ask him/her your questions.

_____

_____

_____

_____

_____

_____

_____

_____

2.   Make a play out of the questions and answers. Perhaps you could have another animal character acting as the reporter. Try writing out the script like this in your copybooks – work as a pair.

Reporter Rat:	What made you go to look for winter?
Winter Hedgehog:	I heard two foxes talking about it and wanted to see it for myself...

B. Word trap – saw/seen

⭐ **Definition box**

A verb is an action word.

Here are two verbs that we sometimes mix up.

| saw | seen |

Example
The winter hedgehog saw a fox on the river bank.
The fox had seen the hedgehog too.

---

1. Mark these sentences correct or incorrect.   Correct Incorrect
    1. I seen the moon up in the sky last night.
    2. The hedgehog thought he had been saw by the fox.
    3. Quick! Run! We have been seen by the teacher!
    4. I saw a great film on TV last night.
    5. I will tell the teacher what I have saw.
    6. I have saw lots of wild animal programmes on TV.
    7. Have you saw the new Batman movie?
    8. I seen the Eiffel Tower when I was on holidays in Paris.

2. Edit the incorrect sentences and rewrite them in your copybook.

3. Add saw or seen to the sentences below.

    1. The little boy knew he had been _____.

    2. I had _____ that TV programme before.

    3. Perfect Peter _____ that Horrid Henry could be good.

    4. The ghost _____ everybody but he could not be _____.

    5. I _____ the burglar trying to break into the house and I told the

       Garda what I had _____.

    6. The hedgehog _____ the world in its winter cloak.

4.   Put in see, saw or seen to complete these sentences. Then write the answer.

1. Did you __see__ that? *Yes, I saw that.*

2. Have you _____ any good films recently? _____
   _____

3. Do you think we were _____ by the teacher? _____
   _____

4. Do you think you will _____ your Granny tomorrow? _____
   _____

5. When is the last time you _____ your friend Michael? _____
   _____

Hedgehogs

A. Woodland creatures

1.   Do you know your woodland animals? Un-jumble these to find the names of some woodland creatures.

tsaot		inkm	
qurirsle		olme	
dabreg		abbrti	
xfo		edheggoh	

2.   Now write a short sentence to describe each of these woodland creatures.

A fox is like a small dog with red fur and a bushy tail.
_____
_____
_____
_____
_____
_____
_____

B. Comparisons

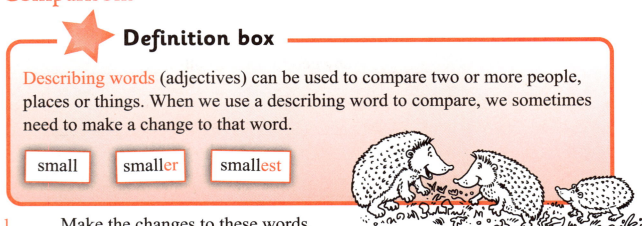

Definition box

Describing words (adjectives) can be used to compare two or more people, places or things. When we use a describing word to compare, we sometimes need to make a change to that word.

small   smaller   smallest

1. Make the changes to these words.

cold	**colder**	**coldest**
dark	_____	_____
fast	_____	_____
long	_____	_____
sharp	_____	_____
warm	_____	_____
soft	_____	_____
old	_____	_____
high	_____	_____

2. Choose five of the word groups you have made to write sentences in your copybook like this.

   Today is cold, yesterday was colder but last Sunday was the coldest day of all.

3. Complete the following sentences.

   1. My Dad has an _____ record but he swapped it for an _____ one.

   2. The pond is _____ but the lake is _____ still.

   3. The motorbike was _____ but the car was even _____.

   4. It took a _____ time to drive to Wexford but even _____ to drive to Cork.

   5. Spring is _____ but summer is _____.

   6. Carrauntoohil is _____ but Everest is even _____.

   7. A knife is _____ but a razor is even _____.

4.   We often compare things by adding the word endings (suffixes) –er or –est to words. But this doesn't always work. For example, read the sentence below.

This is a beautiful flower, here is a beautifuler flower, but this one is the beautifulest of all.

That doesn't sound right! See if you can correct the sentence.

_____

_____

Think of five other describing words where it would be wrong to add –er or –est and list these in your copybook.

C. Prefixes

1.   Put five of these words into sentences.

mystery	uncanny	puzzled	twitched	sniff
unexpectedly	handkerchief	jersey	impatient	idiot

1. _____

2. _____

3. _____

4. _____

5. _____

2.   Two of these words, uncanny and unexpectedly, have the same prefix, un-. Use your dictionary to find other words that begin with this prefix. Write the words that you find in the boxes below.

3.   Choose five of the words you have discovered and use them in sentences.

1. _____

2. _____

3. _____

4. _____

5. _____

Clever challenges

1. Make a fact map about another woodland creature in this box. Use the same headings the author used in the fact map about the hedgehog in your Anthology (page 70).

2. The story begins with a description of an autumn afternoon – *One cold, misty autumn afternoon, the hedgehogs gathered in the wood.* Write six other describing sentences you could start a story with.

> **Examples**
> ■ One sunny, glorious summer morning, the children gathered on the beach.
> ■ One icy, freezing winter day, the penguins gathered on the iceberg.

3. Pick one of the story starters you made up and finish the story.

4. Write the story *The Winter Hedgehog* from the fox's point of view into your copybook. Do not forget to plan it first.
   Read your story to a friend and then to the class.

Weather

Weather facts

1. Someone did not read the piece on weather in the Anthology carefully enough and got their facts wrong. Rewrite the sentences correctly.

1. A tornado once sucked up 12 clowns in India. _____
   _____

2. A shower of toads once fell on a city in Scotland. _____
   _____

3. The biggest snowflakes ever recorded fell in Pakistan, near India.
   _____

4. A hurricane once plucked all the feathers off a flock of geese. _____
   _____

5. A shower of gold coins once fell in Brazil._____
   _____

6. A giant rainbow lasted for five hours over Northern Ireland._____
   _____

2. Draw a picture of one of the amazing weather facts you have read about in your Anthology.

This picture shows _____

What is Fog?

Look back on the poem in your Anthology to fill in the blank spaces below. At the end, make up one sentence of your own to describe fog.

1. The fog was so thick it was like puffs of _____ from a dragon's mouth.

2. It was hard to drive because the fog was _____ round the roads and ditches.

3. The fog in the city was like clouds of _____ from a giant kettle.

4. The fog made the whole world into one grey _____.

5. The thick fog was like the breath from a dinosaur's _____.

6. _____

   _____

Clever challenges

1. Do some research to find other old sayings or folklore about the weather like the ones you read about in your Anthology. Ask your parents or grandparents if they know of any.

   > **Example**
   > Rain before seven, fine by eleven.

2. What interesting verbs you can find in the poem 'The Wild Wind'! Read the verbs below then choose five and write a sentence of your own for each of them.

   > sweeping swerving snatching whisk whistling whooshing
   > sniffing snapping shattering swirling twirling whirling

Real Dragons Roar

Word bank

dragon narrator kingdom ordinary scaly fudge selfish bored highness fed up hopeless hide and seek miserable concerned popped rescued maiden distress nowadays knight hero famous meanwhile groom saddle rumbling chess challenge seize darning dreadful delighted terrify frightening roar breath disappeared arrow sword well bucket velvet concentrate old-fashioned sensible

A. A famous dragon

One of the most famous dragons in literature is 'Smaug'. He is a character in the novel *The Hobbit*, written by J.R.R. Tolkien. In this extract, the hobbit, Bilbo Baggins, meets Smaug for the first time. He has come to steal some of the dragon's treasure (Oh, and by the way he is wearing a magic ring that makes him invisible – the famous one from *Lord of the Rings*).

> *There he lay, a vast red-golden dragon, fast asleep… Beneath him, under all his limbs and his huge coiled tail, and about him on all sides stretching away across the unseen floors, lay countless piles of precious things, gold wrought and unwrought, gems and jewels, and silver red-stained in the ruddy light.*

Imagine the dragon sleeping on his treasure hoard. Now create a new picture of this scene in the box below.

B. Dictionary work

Look at the list of words from *Real Dragons Roar* in your Anthology. Guess what each means first and then look up the meaning in your dictionary.

Word	I think it means	The dictionary says
scaly		
concerned		
distress		
maiden		
narrator		
concentrate		
hopeless		
darning		

C. Different types of writing

Rewrite the first part of the play as a *narrative* piece (in the form of a story).

Once upon a time, long ago, in a faraway kingdom, there lived a dragon. He was not the usual kind of dragon because he was friendly. He didn't even breathe fire when strangers walked past his cave. He didn't even smoke. He wore socks because he didn't want his sharp claws to hurt anyone.

_____

_____

_____

_____

_____

_____

_____

_____

_____

_____

_____

_____

_____

_____ She made very good fudge!

Clever challenges

1. You are the producer of the play 'Real Dragons Roar'. Make up a storyboard with nine boxes and complete it by drawing a scene in each box to tell the story.

2. Draw a map showing the places where the action takes place and label them.

3. Choose three characters from your book that you would like to meet. Think of three questions you would like to ask them. Invite three friends in your class to act the parts. Hot seat the characters and ask them your questions.

4. Add drawings to the illustration below to show some of the dragon's friends.

Records in the world of nature

A. Memory check

Answer these questions using full sentences.

1. What is the smallest mammal in the world? _____
   _____

2. Which animal lives longer than any other animal? _____
   _____

3. Were dinosaurs the largest animals that ever lived? _____
   _____

4. Which animal is the smelliest of all? _____
   _____

5. Which animal has the largest eyes? _____
   _____

6. What is the largest bird in the world? _____
   _____

B. Picture research

Find pictures of three of the animals featured in your Anthology. Look for them in magazines or on the Internet. Glue and label the pictures in the spaces below.

☽ Clever challenges

Find a copy of a book such as *The Guinness Book of Records* and scan it for eight interesting records from the natural world. Write them into your copybook.

Dino Egg

Word bank

clambering stench profile tibia formation palaeontologist deceased defunct extinct mutant hesitated lolling quavered saliva herbivores whimpered carnivores gibbering famished fossil obsessed

A. Dino menu

Create a menu for a day to feed little Dino his breakfast, lunch and dinner.

BREAKFAST

LUNCH

DINNER

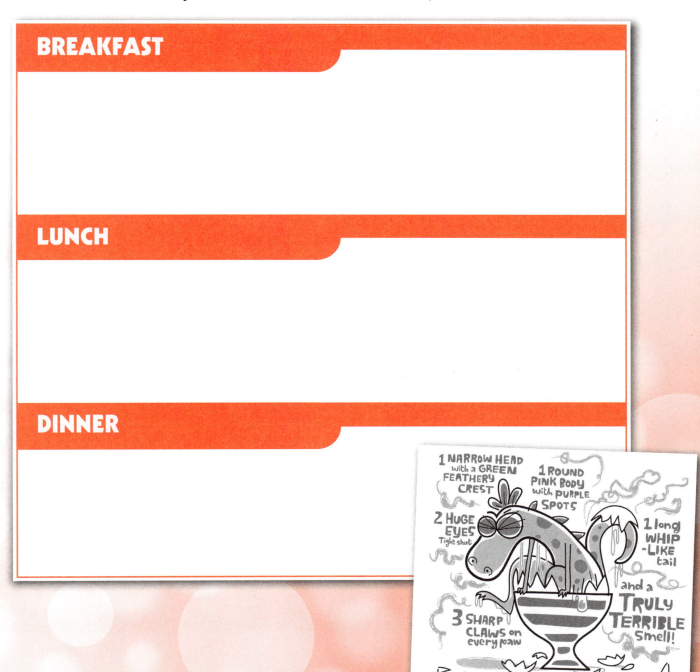

B. Recipe

Write out the ingredients and the method for preparing one of the meals you created in Dino's food diary. Do not forget that there are huge amounts needed to feed a dinosaur.

RECIPE

Ingredients	Method

C. *Dino Egg* questions

1.   This time around the authors got very lazy and didn't finish their work at all. Complete the questions they meant to write about *Dino Egg*.

1.   Who _____

2.   What _____

3.   Where _____

4.   When_____

5.   Why_____

6.   Which _____

7.   Did _____

8.   Do you think _____

2.   Give your set of questions to a friend and ask them to write out the answers in her/his copybook.

D. Compound words

Definition box

You can make a new word by joining two smaller words together. This new word is called a compound word.

Example
Class + room = classroom

1. Join a word in list A with a word in list B to form compound words. Write these words.

List A	List B	Compound words
hair	thing	
every	market	
out	light	
black	side	
super	spray	
some	body	
day	board	
sea	stretched	

2. Make your own list of nine compound words.

_____	_____	_____
_____	_____	_____
_____	_____	_____

3. Put each word in a sentence to show you know what it means.

_____

_____

_____

_____

_____

_____

_____

_____

E. Contractions

 Definition box

Sometimes we take short cuts in writing. We drop a letter or letters and make one word out of two. This is called a contraction.

Example

do + not = don't	we + are = we're	I + am = I'm
did + not = didn't	I + will = I'll	it + is = it's

1. Match these words with their short cuts.

do not	can't
I will	it's
cannot	we're
it is	wasn't
were not	don't
was not	weren't
we are	I'll

2. Rewrite these sentences using short cuts.

1. When I grow up, I will be an accountant. _____
_____

2. Tomorrow we will go to the circus. _____
_____

3. When I am on holidays, I do not have to do homework. _____
_____

4. She did not eat her dinner. _____
_____

5. 'Do not fry those sausages,' Mum said. _____
_____

3. Read the story of Dino again and list all the short cuts you can find.

_____   _____   _____

_____   _____   _____

_____   _____   _____

4. Now write them as two separate words.

_____   _____   _____   _____

_____   _____   _____   _____

_____   _____   _____   _____

_____   _____   _____   _____

_____   _____

F. Storyboard

Tell the story of *Dino Egg* in a storyboard using pictures and short sentences only.

The shell split open...

G. Dino poem

Sometimes writing a poem is easier if you have help. Use these starter lines to write your own poem about Dino and what he liked.

Dino's Likes

Dino liked to _____.

Dino liked to _____.

Dino liked to _____.

Dino liked to _____.

Dino liked to _____.

Dino liked to _____.

Dino liked to _____.

Dino liked to _____.

Dino liked to _____.

Dino liked to _____.

Dino liked to _____.

Dino liked to _____.

Now share your poems with a partner and then with the class. Make a class book of dino poems. Illustrate the poems and the book cover using lots of colour.

Dinosaurs

1.   Answer these questions in your copybook using
      full sentences.

   1. Could a caveman have met a dinosaur? Explain your answer.

   2. What is the difference between a carnivore and a herbivore?

   3. Are human beings carnivores, omnivores or herbivores?

   4. What is a fossil? Explain.

   5. What was the first dinosaur fossil ever found?

   6. Why did meat-eating dinosaurs hunt in packs?

   7. How did the stegosaurus defend itself?

   8. What kind of food do you think a brachiosaurus mainly ate and why?

   9. Why do scientists think the dinosaurs became extinct?

   10. What was unusual about the gallimimus?

2.   A *lexicon* is a list in alphabetical order. Remember the chart on the classroom
      wall when you were learning the alphabet? Each letter had a picture opposite of
      something beginning with that letter. For example A = picture of an apple. Now
      create a dinosaur lexicon. Start with the information piece in your Anthology
      and then research other dinosaur names or things associated with dinosaurs (for
      example, fossil) to make a list. Begin like this:

   ■ A Allosaurus   ■ N _____
   ■ B Brontosaurus   ■ O _____
   ■ C _____   ■ P _____
   ■ D _____   ■ Q _____
   ■ E _____   ■ R _____
   ■ F _____   ■ S _____
   ■ G _____   ■ T _____
   ■ H _____   ■ U _____
   ■ I _____   ■ V _____
   ■ J _____   ■ W _____
   ■ K _____   ■ X _____
   ■ L _____   ■ Y _____
   ■ M _____   ■ Z _____

3.   Work as a class to create a lexicon to put on the wall of your classroom.

Two poems

Which of the two dinosaur poems in the Anthology do you prefer? Draw a cartoon illustration for your favourite here. Show your cartoon to your friends. Ask them to guess which poem you chose.

 Clever challenges

1. Imagine you are the family dog in *Dino Egg*. Tell the story *Dino Egg* from the time the shell cracked open.

2. You are a local journalist. Think of questions you need to ask to write a report on this story. Then write it up in your copybook.

3. What do you think will happen next in the story? Write about it.

4. Think of a day in your life and the food you eat. Complete the same table as on page 63 for your breakfast, lunch and dinner.

5. Compare your daily food diary with a partner in your class.

6. Do a small project on dinosaurs. Use the Internet and your library to find information.

Specky Becky Bucks

 Word bank

exhibition blurted concerned scuttling minors heroes injuries curious hydrangeas savage target shimmy praising avoid ruffled business explained state sighed

A. Verbs

 Definition box

Reminder: Verbs are action words. Every sentence needs a verb. It tells us what action takes place.

Example
We sat on a bench in the park watching squirrels scuttling across the grass.

1. Choose a suitable verb for each of these sentences.

   1. An old man _____ in horror as the burglar climbed in through the window.

   2. Pat _____ crossly that he had left his homework on the bus.

   3. The teacher _____ wearily when the tests were corrected.

   4. My baby brother suddenly _____ out the secret to Dad.

   5. 'Becky, you must hold on to your dreams,' _____ Grandad.

   6. The footballer ran towards the goal but was _____ by a player from the other team.

2. Verbs or action words describe what the characters in the story are up to. Check the stories in your Anthology and write out six sentences that tell us what the characters are doing.

   _____

   _____

   _____

   _____

   _____

   _____

B. Singular and plural

Definition box

Sometimes when we change from singular to plural, we need to look at the rules, for example, changing y to i and adding es.

Example
injury injuries
body bodies

Change these sentences from singular to plural.

1. My fabulous granny came to visit my school to talk to my class. _____
   _____

2. The child used the computer to write the story of the Famine for homework. _____
   _____

3. The pupil fell as she brought her copy up to the teacher._____
   _____

4. 'I lost my teddy,' whispered the little boy. _____
   _____

Clever challenges

1. 'The Future is Now' Exhibition is coming to your school. You are helping to organise it. Draw up the programme giving all the information about the displays. Plan your ideas first in your copybook. Use the computer to print your programme.

Checklist – Make sure to include		
✓ Title of exhibition	✓ Place	✓ Areas of display
✓ Illustration	✓ Time	✓ Things on display in
✓ Date		each area

2. Send an invitation to a grandparent or older member of your family asking them to visit your classroom.

3. Make up questions you want to ask them about exciting times in their lives when they were younger.

4. Write out one of the stories they tell you.

5. 'Well, you just hold on to your dreams... you never know!' – Grandad gave good advice to Becky. What is your dream? Make a map of the steps you will take to make your dream come true.

The Moon

Features of the moon

1. Many years ago, when people thought there was life on the moon, they gave interesting names to certain features there, for example, *The Sea of Tranquility*. Find out the names of other features on the moon.

_____   _____

_____   _____

_____   _____

_____   _____

2. Draw a map or diagram of our solar system here.

The Legend of the Worst Boy in the World

Word bank

complaining generally moaning actual hangnail hobby horses whinging whines
entertaining chuckles sulking hallucinations efficiently patience tattoo perched miracle
reckoned

A. Problems, problems

1. Will tells us a lot about his brothers' problems. He thinks there are *actual* problems and *silly* problems.

   Make a list of the *actual* and *silly* problems you have with your brothers/sisters **or** of the *actual* and *silly* problems you find in your class.

Actual problems	Silly problems

2. What is your daily moan at home or at school? Write it as a four-line poem.

   _____

   _____

   _____

   _____

3. Share your moans with a partner. Make a Class Moan Book.

B. Add-ing

skip		feel	
read		chat	
cut		break	
hop		teach	
clean		tap	
sit		dig	

C. Word trap – were/where

Complete the sentences using were or where.

1. Will's problems _____ real problems, his brothers' problems _____ silly.

2. Bert and HP knew _____ Mum kept the cookies.

3. Will and Marty _____ sure Grandad would listen to their problems.

4. '_____ are we going to get a full-sized snooker table?' asked Will's Dad.

5. We _____ all very happy when we had no homework.

6. The pirate knew _____ the treasure was buried before he set sail for the island.

D. Word work

Sometimes we make up new words. They are not in the dictionary but we use them all the same. Bert and HP have new words to help them whinge all the better.

Think up brand new words that would grab Mum or Dad's attention and say what they mean by completing the table below.

Brand new word	Meaning

Clever challenges

1. Your parents want to present you with a cardboard OSCAR. This is an award for something you are good at. What would it be for? Write the speech they would give. Ask them to help you with this exercise.

2. A hobby horse is something you feel very strongly about. It could be something you want to change or stop like whale hunting. Write a paragraph to convince a friend to 'get off his/her hobby horse'. Plan your ideas first.

3. Poor Donnie has 'hair hallucinations'. This is his 'hobby horse'– his hair is never right. Tell what happened the day you had a hair hallucination. Illustrate your bad hair day in the mirror.

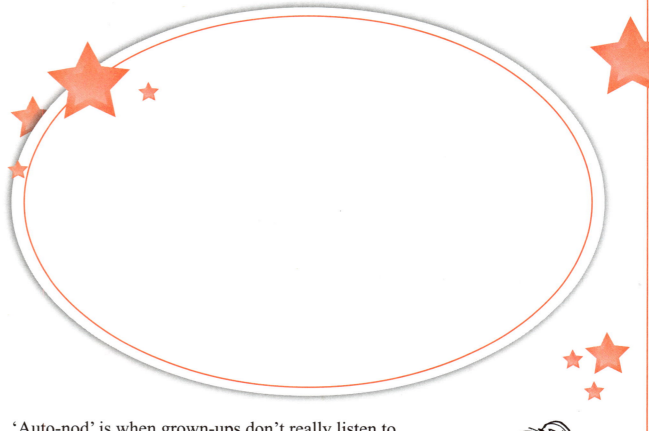

4. 'Auto-nod' is when grown-ups don't really listen to what a child says, they just nod every five seconds until the child goes away. Is this a good or bad thing? Explain.

Judy Moody Saves the World!

Word bank

garbage recycled rainforest plunger pollution chainsaw oatmeal detective compost museum kindling trudged sloth grinding clomped oxygen kindergarten complicated

A. Adjectives

Definition box

Adjectives tell us more about nouns. They are used to describe a noun.

Example
The old, grey dog looked over the garden wall.
The red, crispy leaves crunched under my feet.

1. Match the nouns in list A with the adjectives in List B.

Nouns	Adjectives
waves	clever
snake	angry
bird	booming
dog	crashing
girl	slithering
thunder	chirpy

2. Write a sentence using each pair of words above.

_____

_____

_____

_____

_____

_____

3. Make a list of nouns in your copybook. Swap with your partner and find adjectives to match the nouns.

B. Mister Rubbish

1. Mr Rubbish was the good Garbage Gremlin in Stink's comic book. He made things from recycled materials. Make a list of recycled materials you can find at home and in school.

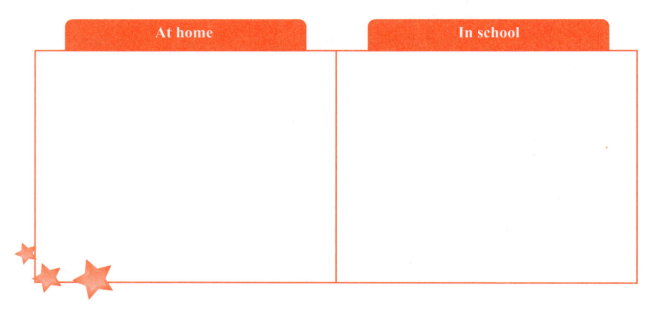

At home	In school

2. Design something useful that can be made from some or all of these things. Draw your design here.

3. Write a description of the design in your copybook.

4. Judy wished to save the rainforest. Look back on the story where she lists the things her family use or do that damage this ecosystem. Write down the points she might have made at the Family Meeting to make them change their ways.

_____

_____

_____

_____

5. For homework, start your own PROJECT RECYCLE. Make a list of all the things your family throws away in a week. You may have to be a Garbage Detective.

Project recycle list

_____

_____

_____

_____

_____

_____

_____

_____

_____

_____

_____

_____

_____

_____

_____

C. Occupations

Judy was a garbage detective or a 'garbologist'. Complete this list of other *occupations* or jobs. Use a dictionary to help you.

Name	Job
Chemist	A person who...
Carpenter	A person who...
Journalist	A person who...
Plumber	A person who...
Vet	A person who...
Clown	A person who...
Astronaut	A person who...

Clever challenges

1. Design a poster to hang in the kitchen or in your classroom to remind everyone of Judy's ideas about saving the world.

2. Read the story of Judy Moody again. What words would you use to describe her character? Working with a partner, list six of these adjectives in your copybook.

3. Judy wished she could recycle her little brother Stink. If you could recycle someone from your family, who would it be? Write a report on what you would do.

Word bank

awful nature keeper recognised matter immediately represented reason engineer contained fierce padlocked tetanus blood poisoning ferociously yardman stroking woolly snarled leash harvest vacation canvas station wagon fastener disturb

A. Pets

Read the poem.

I Have a Lion

Karla Kuskin

I had a cat,
grey
soft
fat
given to grrrrring
quite softly
and prrrrring.
Slipped off one morning
near the green glen.
That was my cat
who was not seen again.

I had a dog,
noisy and yellow
very cold nose
wonderful fellow.
Trotted one evening
out after a pack
of dog-footed friends
and never came back.

I had a bird,
bright blue in a cage
sang without cease
on his miniature stage.
Sat on my shoulder
looked in my eye
sailed out the window
and into the sky.

I have a lion,
furry and kind
sits on a shelf
near the autos that wind.
Eyes wild and golden
tail like a tuft
he never will slip out and leave me.
He's stuffed.

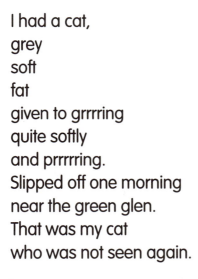

1. In the poem 'I Have a Lion' the writer describes her pets. Three are real animals, one is a toy. List the problems the writer might have had if the toy pet were real!

Problems

1. _____

2. _____

3. _____

2. Make two lists, one for animals or birds that you think make good pets and one for those that would not.

Good pets	Not so good pets
kittens	crocodiles

3. Write a sentence to explain why you put one of the animals in the second box in there.

_____

_____

_____

B. Researching cats

1. Name other members of the cat family. Describe them and write what you know about them.

_____

_____

_____

2. Un-jumble the names of the members of the cat family in the box below and write them into your copybook. Use your dictionary, an encyclopedia or the Internet to find an interesting piece of information on them and then write a sentence about each one.

giter	ynxl	eetchha	ionl
naphtre	poelrda	umap	ionl ountmani

C. Agree or disagree

Sometimes we do not agree with what other people think. We should be able to give reasons for this. Wild animals from all over the world are kept in zoos but some people believe that this is wrong. Have a class discussion about zoos. Give three reasons why you agree that zoos are good places for wild animals and three reasons why you disagree (note down keywords).

I disagree because	I agree because
_____	_____
_____	_____
_____	_____

D. Word trap – there/their

Here are two words that we sometimes mix up.

there   their

Example
There were lots of animals in the zoo.
Mark and Catherine were visiting the zoo with their parents.

1. Now see if you can use them correctly.

   1. The animals were in _____ cages in the zoo.

   2. _____ was a huge bed of beautiful flowers.

   3. The birds went on with _____ endless pecking.

   4. The monkeys combed _____ babies' fur with _____ fingers.

   5. _____ was a long slim snake in the snake house.

   6. 'The South American wildcat is in _____,' said the keeper.

2. Correct these sentences and write them in your copybook.

   1. Have they done there homework yet?
   2. Their is a huge spider in that web.
   3. The children will get wet in the rain without there raincoats.
   4. Sit over their beside the fire to get warm.
   5. The passengers put there luggage on the racks overhead.

E. Word trap – to/two/too

Here are three other words that we sometimes mix up.

| to | two | too |

> **Example**
> Mark brought the bag back to the car.
> The bag was big enough for two families.
> It was big enough to hold the lion cub too.

1. Now see if you can use them correctly.
   1. Mark and Catherine went _____ the zoo yesterday.
   2. The keeper took them _____ the snake house.
   3. The _____ children were afraid of the snakes.
   4. Catherine went _____ the cage and saw _____ monkeys.
   5. _____ cages in the monkey house were empty and _____ cages in the lion house were empty _____.
   6. Their parents liked the lions but they liked the tigers _____.
   7. The _____ children saw the lion cub and their parents saw it _____.
   8. 'I'll let you _____ take the cub for a walk,' said the keeper _____ Mark and Catherine.

2. Correct these sayings. Write them in your copybook and explain what each one means.
   1. A bird in the hand is worth too in the bush.
   2. It is better two have loved and lost than never too have loved at all.
   3. To wrongs do not make a right.

Clever challenges

1. Make an alphabetical list of the first names of your classmates.

2. If you were to save the world where would you start? What would you do? Write your ideas down and read them to the class.

3. Write a Green School motto for your school.

4. Have a debate in your class on one of these topics:
   - 'It is wrong to cut down forests.'
   - 'It is wrong to keep animals in zoos.'
   Half of the class must argue for the topic and half must argue against the topic. Your teacher can be the chairperson. Remember to give every pupil a chance to speak. Have a vote on which side made the best arguments.

The human body

Correct sentences

Someone was writing sentences from the text but has added an extra word to each sentence. Can you find the word that does not belong in each sentence and cross it out so that the sentences make sense? Write five of the corrected sentences in your copybook.

1. A baby has over 300 bones muscles when it is born.
2. Three quarters of a human body brain is made of water.
3. You should would use a handkerchief if you sneeze.
4. The brain sends messages to one all parts of the body along the spine.
5. There are about 9000 taste sense buds on your tongue.
6. You should always never look directly at the sun.
7. The heart pumps oxygen air to all parts of your body.
8. Bone cells last for 20 years, skin cells last mend about six weeks.
9. Taste buds can taste sweet, bitter, sour, foul and salty tastes.
10. Your eyes move more than 10,000 times a day hour.

Mark's Fingers

Verbs

Add a verb (doing word) at the end of each finger to tell what your hands can do.

Utterly me, Clarice Bean

Word bank

exhibits habits wallabies probability concentrate hippopotamus dreary obviously citizen responsible abide supervision lodged elaborate discreetly enquired evasively engrossed butler sideline invention formula volcano tapioca

A. Clarice's quiz

Hello everyone. I am Clarice Bean. Read my story in your Anthology and answer the following questions about me and my life.

1. Why am I not talking about my exhibit? _____

   _____

2. Name my best friend who is absent from school. _____

   _____

3. Who is my favourite author? _____

   _____

4. Why did I like having Mrs Nesbit as my teacher? _____

   _____

5. What does Mrs Marse look like, according to me?_____

   _____

6. What terrible deed has Ralph done? _____

   _____

7. Why do I think the postcard might be from Betty? _____

   _____

B. Looking closely at the story

1. Scan the text and find eight words beginning with 'e'. List the words below.

My 'e' word list			

2. Rewrite the list in alphabetical order.

   _____   _____   _____

   _____   _____   _____

   _____   _____

C. Syllable count

Some words can be broken up into different parts or syllables. If we clap as we say the word it helps us to hear how many syllables or sounds are in the words.

Scan the text of this story. Find words in this piece with three syllables or sounds.

> **Example**
> visiting   vis/it/ing

1.   Now, with the words you have selected, become a syllable or sound detective. Ask a partner to help you.

Word	Syllable 1	Syllable 2	Syllable 3
visiting	vis	it	ing

2.   Choose ten more words from any story in your Anthology. Show how these can be broken into syllables in your copybook using a different colour for each syllable.

D. Letter writing

Write a letter to one of your favourite authors. Compare letters with your friends in class.

E. Quick sketches

Draw a quick sketch of each of these characters based on what you have read about them in Clarice Bean's story.

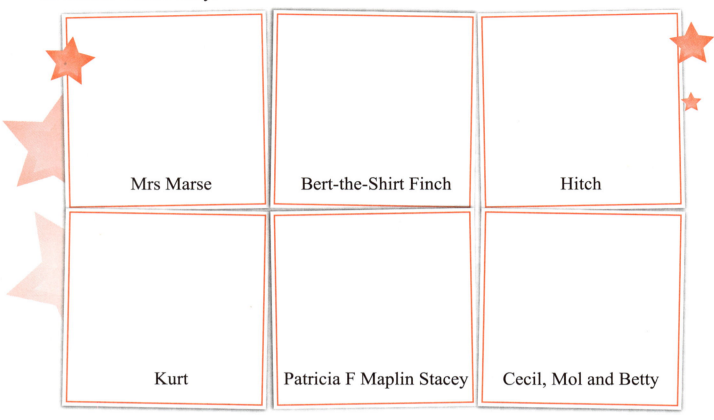

Mrs Marse

Bert-the-Shirt Finch

Hitch

Kurt

Patricia F Maplin Stacey

Cecil, Mol and Betty

F. Write a poem

Write an acrostic poem about:

C_____

L_____

A_____

R_____

I_____

C_____

E_____

B_____

E_____

A_____

N_____

Clever challenges

1. Clarice mentions her book project or exhibit. Your class is having a special display day for each pupil to show their exhibit. What would your one be? Use a sheet to create your exhibit.

2. You have read about different codes in your Anthology. Create a code for responsible citizens.

3. Use the same code as a base for a School Code.

4. Design and make a poster of your code for display in the school corridor.

5. Invent your own code and send messages using this code to your friends. Did they find it hard or easy to decode your message?

6. Look at how the author Lauren Child illustrates her work. Find more of her books and note the style she mainly uses for her illustrations. Cut out pictures from magazines and stick them here. Then add to them by drawing.

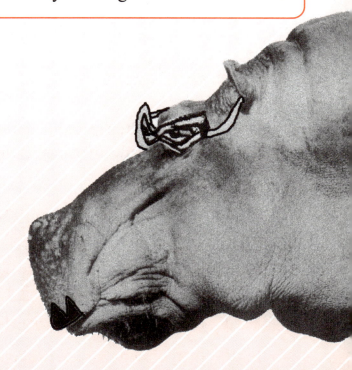

You're a Bad Man, Mr Gum!

Word bank

bloodshot octopus complete corn on the cob snoozing scowling townsfolk slime disgusting pigsty junk pizza wounded cupboard absolutely grimsters mould moth-eaten duvet assembling chucked dumped ancient lazer crocuses daffodils launderette whacking whopper

A. Messy!

1. Mr Gum's house is like a pigsty. Describe the most untidy room in your house.

_____

_____

_____

_____

_____

_____

_____

_____

2. The health inspector came to visit Mr Gum. In your copybook write the report he/she made after inspecting his house.

B. Headlines

The old newspapers in Mr Gum's house contained headlines from many years ago.

VIKINGS INVADE IRELAND

1. In your copybook write five headlines from history like the one above.
2. Write five headlines from the local paper about Mr Gum's house and garden.
3. Choose one headline for homework and write the newspaper report to match it.

C. Cartoons

Make a cartoon version of the chapter you have just read from Mr Gum's story.

Mr Gum was a fierce old man.	He snoozed all day in bed.	His house was like a disgusting pigsty.
His bedroom was absolutely grimsters.	His garden was amazing.	An angry fairy would whack him with a pan.

Clever challenges

1. A little child wanders into Mr Gum's garden. Imagine how he might have reacted to her/him. Write out the script for a play between the two characters.

2. Choose any two stories from the Anthology that you think were much the same or very different. Compare the two stories you chose in your copybook using the following chart.

Name of story:	Main characters:
Type of story:	Character descriptions:
I liked/did not like it because:	

3. Read the clues! Which characters from the Anthology are being described here? Fill in the characters' names.

She had golden hair. _____

Her Grandad got into trouble at the old folk's home. _____

This boy threw a plate of spaghetti. _____

A man with two bloodshot eyes. _____

She often had her nose stuck in a book. _____

Uncle Frederic told her not to be foolish. _____

Her uncle is called Mitchell. _____

This creature went to find winter. _____

His youngest brother is nicknamed Half Pint. _____

The boys who broke the kitchen window. _____

She plans to save the world. _____

This character had a pet baby dinosaur. _____

Her Grandad had been a bus driver in London. _____

Who had a surprise in his picnic bag? _____

4. Create your own character search in your copybook/using a word programme. Give it to a partner to complete.